Spotlight

Plays for the ESOL Classroom

THE NECKLACE

Spotlight

Titles available in the series

THE WALL

based on "The Great Whitewasher"
from *The Adventures of Tom Sawyer*
by Mark Twain

10,000 BASKETS

based on "Assembly Line"
a short story by B. Traven

THE NECKLACE

based on "The Necklace"
a short story by Guy de Maupassant

THE COWBOY AND THE WILDCAT

based on "The Taming of the Shrew"
by William Shakespeare

Spotlight

Plays for the ESOL Classroom

THE NECKLACE

Based on "The Necklace"
a short story by Guy de Maupassant

Lonnie Burstein Hewitt
San Diego Community College

Penny Bernal
San Dieguito High School
and
Palomar Community College

McGraw Hill, Inc.
New York   St. Louis   San Francisco   Auckland   Bogotà   Caracas
Lisbon   London   Madrid   Mexico City   Milan   Montreal   New Delhi
San Juan   Singapore   Sydney   Tokyo   Toronto

SPOTLIGHT: PLAYS FOR THE ESOL CLASSROOM

The Necklace

This book is printed on recycled, acid-free paper
containing 10% postconsumer waste.

1 2 3 4 5 6 7 8 9 0 DOC DOC 9 0 9 8 7 6 5

ISBN 0-07-009252-4

This book was set in Melior and Syntax by Professional Book Center.
The editors were Tim Stookesberry and Suzanne Thibodeau; the
design was done by Professional Book Center; the illustrations were
drawn by Dick Ayers; the cover was designed by Karen K. Quigley; the
production supervisor was Phil Galea. Project supervision was done
by Professional Book Center. R. R. Donnelley & Sons Company was
printer and binder.

Library of Congress Cataloging-in-Publication Data

Hewitt, Lonnie Burstein, (date).
    The necklace: based on The necklace, a short story by Guy de
Maupassant / Lonnie Burstein Hewitt, Penny Bernal.
        p.   cm. — (Spotlight)
    ISBN 0-07-009252-4
    1. English language—Textbooks for foreign speakers. 2. Drama in
    education. 3. Readers—Drama. I. Bernal, Penny. II. Maupassant,
    Guy de, 1850–1893. Parure. III. Title. IV. Series: Hewitt, Lonnie
    Burstein, (date). Spotlight.
    PE1128.H43542   1995
    428.6'4—dc20   94-33729

ABOUT THE AUTHORS

Lonnie Burstein Hewitt has taught English as a Second Language (ESL) for over a decade at San Diego Community College. Prior to that, she acted, directed, and wrote for the theater in New York, and designed acting and writing programs for schools and hospitals. She has written plays for Broadway, songs for "Sesame Street," and numerous newspaper articles and book reviews. She is also coauthor of a popular nature/history guidebook, *Walking San Diego.*

Penny Bernal has been an ESL teacher for 15 years and is currently chairperson of the ESL department at San Dieguito High School in San Diego. She also teaches writing at Palomar Community College. A specialist in drama activities for the ESL classroom, she is a frequent speaker and consultant at ESL and multicultural conferences. She has been a mentor teacher in her district and a fellow in the San Diego Area Writing Project.

Penny Bernal (left) and Lonnie Burstein Hewitt

This book is dedicated to our students and students everywhere who are bravely exploring the weird and wonderful world of the English language.

CONTENTS

DEAR READER:

The plays in our series are based on classic stories, but they are written in the kind of real-life American English that people today actually speak. Think of them as *your* plays, written just for *you.*

Don't be afraid to suggest extra lines and actions for your favorite characters. Try adding expressions from your own language and culture to make our plays more personal. Maybe your class can perform one of the plays in front of an audience. Maybe you want to try writing a play of your own.

Whatever you do, enjoy it. These books are meant to be fun!

If after reading or acting in our plays, you would like to share your experiences with us, please write to us in care of our publisher. We'd love to hear from you.

A play is never complete without an audience. Thank you for being ours.

Sincerely,

Lonnie & Penny

Lonnie & Penny

ACKNOWLEDGMENTS

Our thanks to all those who gave us support and suggestions when we needed them most:

■ Our colleagues and friends, especially Sue Raley, Catherine Close, and Dianne Frost of the San Dieguito District; and Cindy Wislofsky, San Diego Community College ESL Department Chair Extraordinaire; also Bernice Glenn, perpetual sounding board; Richard Hastings, music consultant; and Susan Green, photographer.

■ Our families, especially Lonnie's mother, Mickey Burstein, for a lifetime of loving encouragement, and husband Maurice Hewitt, for always being there; and Penny's husband, Ralph Bernal, and children, Nick and Jolie, for their infinite patience while Mom worked on the books.

■ Our reviewers, whose thoughtful comments helped shape this project: Laurie Edwards, College of Lake County; Jas Gill, University of British Columbia; Stacy Hagan, Edmonds Community College; Patricia Johnson, Dunbar Language School; Philip Plourde, Southern Illinois University, Carbondale; and Robin Roy, Olney High School.

■ Our friends at McGraw-Hill: Thalia Dorwick, Bill Preston, and Suzanne Thibodeau for their insightful guidance; Margaret Metz and the entire McGraw-Hill sales staff for their tireless promotional efforts; and especially our editor, the incomparable Tim Stookesberry, whose interest and enthusiasm made this series possible, and his assistant, the equally enthusiastic and helpful Gina Martinez.

Guy de Maupassant (Bettman)

ABOUT THE ORIGINAL

"The Necklace," written by Guy de Maupassant, is the story of a pretty, self-centered young woman in late nineteenth-century France. Matilde feels cheated by life. She has all the good taste and fine manners of the rich but none of the money. Hoping to make her happy, her husband, a government clerk, brings home an invitation to an elegant party. He even agrees to let her spend all his savings on an evening dress. As a finishing touch, she borrows a beautiful necklace from a wealthy friend.

At the party, Matilde has a wonderful time until she discovers that the necklace is gone. Matilde and her husband borrow money to buy a replacement for the lost necklace and work ten long years to pay back the loans. Hard work destroys Matilde's beauty, but she never forgets that one special night. The story is known for its surprise ending.

Guy de Maupassant (1850–1893) originally wanted to be a lawyer, but couldn't afford to continue his studies. So he began working at a series of government jobs and went on to study writing with the great French author, Flaubert. Unlike most writers, he achieved immediate success and became the most popular short story writer of his time. "The Necklace" is probably his best-known work.

In our play, the details of the original story have changed, but the idea remains the same.

PREVIEWS

SOMETHING TO THINK ABOUT

1. Read the following statements. Do you agree or disagree?
   Check the box to show your answer.

	AGREE	DISAGREE
a. Beautiful people are often cold and unfeeling.	☐	☐
b. Most people believe they deserve more from life.	☐	☐
c. Diamonds are a girl's best friend.	☐	☐
d. Hard work makes you a better person.	☐	☐
e. One unexpected event can change your whole life.	☐	☐

2. Compare your answers with a partner. Discuss your reasons
   for your opinions. Did your partner say anything to change
   your mind?

3. In *The Necklace*, an unexpected event changes the heroine's
   life. Has something like that ever happened to you? What
   was the event? How did it change your life?

KEY WORDS AND EXPRESSIONS

All of the words and expressions below are found in *The Necklace*. Can you guess what they mean?

deserve

fake

glamorous

Give me a hand.

heartbroken

He's not your type.

How come?

(It) costs a fortune.

put up with (someone or something)

lazy

Look me up.

recognize

In the following exercises, circle the correct definition for the underlined word. The first one is done for you.

1. In *The Necklace,* Rosa dreams of a glamorous career as a fashion model. Glamorous means,

    a. relaxing

    b. full of love

    c. fascinating and beautiful

    d. busy and satisfying

2. Someone who says, "Give me a hand," usually wants

    a. applause

    b. help

    c. a hug

    d. your glove

3. A person who says, "Look me up," is asking you to

    a. visit

    b. admire him or her

    c. raise your eyes

    d. pay attention

4. If you put up with a difficult person, it means you
   a. let him or her stay at your house
   b. don't let his or her behavior bother you
   c. climb the stairs together
   d. have an argument

5. He's not your type means he
   a. cannot use your typewriter or computer
   b. is always late
   c. is not your kind of person
   d. knows you can type

6. How come? means
   a. How did you come here?
   b. Why?
   c. Where?
   d. How do you style your hair?

7. Someone who is heartbroken is
   a. very sick
   b. very much in love
   c. very unhappy
   d. recovering from an accident

8. A lazy person
   a. doesn't tell the truth
   b. doesn't like to work
   c. cannot think clearly
   d. moves rapidly

9. Someone who deserves the best,
   a. works in a good restaurant
   b. likes rich desserts
   c. plays tennis well
   d. has a right to the best things in life

10. Anything that is <u>fake</u> is

    a. real

    b. not real

    c. sweet

    b. bitter

11. When you see something you think <u>costs a fortune</u>, it is probably

    a. a piece of music

    b. very cheap

    c. very expensive

    d. someone else's

12. If you don't <u>recognize</u> someone, that person probably

    a. is a friend

    b. is a relative

    c. has given you too much to drink

    d. has changed a lot

HOW TO READ A PLAY

Have you ever read a play before? Since plays are mostly **dialogue,** or conversations, they give a good idea of how people really speak to each other. All you need to know are a few expressions so that you can understand the **stage directions.** Stage directions describe what the **characters**—the people in the play—do, and may also describe where the **action** of the play takes place. Stage directions are generally printed in *italics.*

A long play is divided into **acts,** and the acts are divided into shorter sections called **scenes.** The play you are about to read is a **one-act play.**

Plays are usually performed on a **stage,** which is often a raised platform in a theater. Characters in a play are either **onstage,** where the **audience** watching the play can see them; or **offstage,** where they cannot be seen. As they are needed, characters **enter** or **exit.**

The characters in a play are also called the **cast.** The **main** or **leading characters** are the most important ones. They usually have the most to say. But **minor characters** can be interesting too. **Actors** play the **parts,** or **roles,** in a play. The person who tells them what to do and how to do it is called the **director.** The writer of the play is called the **playwright.** The play itself is often called a **script.**

STAGE DIRECTIONS

In a play, actions help tell the story and are often described in the stage directions. Here are some things the characters do in *The Necklace.* Which of them can you demonstrate? Your teacher will help you with the ones you do not know. With a partner, take turns acting out each one.

1. Stretch
2. Dust
3. Blow a kiss
4. Smooth your hair
5. Balance a book on your head
6. Bump into something
7. Giggle
8. Roll your eyes
9. Groan
10. Shrug
11. Play catch
12. Burst into tears
13. Tiptoe in
14. Yawn
15. Squint
16. Mutter

SPANISH GLOSSARY

The following Spanish words and expressions are used in *The Necklace*. This list shows how to pronounce them and what they mean in English.

SPANISH	PRONOUNCIATION	ENGLISH MEANING
¡Qué bonita eres!	kay bo-NEE-ta AIR-ess	How pretty you are!
¡Qué precioso!	kay pray-see-OH-so	How beautiful!
¡Muchísimas gracias!	moo-CHEE-see-mahss GRAH-see-ahss	Thank you so much!
De nada.	day NAH-dah	You're welcome.
Me llamo . . .	may YAH-mo	My name is . . .
princesa	preen-SAY-sah	princess

How would you say these things in your native language?

ENGLISH	YOUR LANGUAGE
How pretty you are!	_____
How beautiful!	_____
Thank you so much!	_____
You're welcome.	_____
My name is . . .	_____
princess	_____

THE NECKLACE

by Lonnie Burstein Hewitt and Penny Bernal

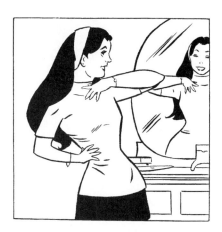

*A pretty, self-centered young woman is forced to change
her life when she loses a borrowed necklace.
(Based on "The Necklace" by Guy de Maupassant.)*

CAST

(in order of appearance)

Rosa López

Michael and *Julie,* two children

Mrs. Kelly, their mother and Rosa's employer

Lily, Roberto, Víctor, Suzi, and *Mr. Santini,*
    English as a Second Language students

Teacher

Waiter

3 *Men* and 3 *Women,* dinner dance guests

SCENE 1

A room in the Kelly house.

[Rosa *enters, wearing a portable tape player with earphones.
She is listening to an English-language tape, repeating each sentence after she hears it. She is holding a feather duster.*]

Rosa: [*Listens, then repeats carefully:*] Good evening. [*Listens
and repeats:*] I am very pleased to meet *you.* [*Listens, starts
to dust the dresser, and repeats:*] May I have this dance?
[*Listens and repeats:*] Certainly.

[*Listens, stops dusting, looks at herself in the imaginary mirror over the dresser, smooths her hair, and repeats:*] Do you
know the fox-trot? . . . *Fox-trot?*

[*She turns off the tape player.*] What's *that?* I'd better look it
up. Here's Mrs. Kelly's dictionary. [*She takes a thick book
from the dresser, admiring herself in the mirror again.*] Oh,
Rosa, ¡qué bonita eres! You look like a model.

[*She blows a kiss at her reflection in the mirror. Then she picks
up the dictionary, balances it on her head, and announces dra-
matically:*]

Here she is, the star of our show, Miss Rosa López! She's wearing the latest fashion from Paris, the "Dictionary Hat"!

[Rosa *turns and begins to walk toward the audience, like a model. Suddenly two children run in, bump into her, and knock the book off her head.*]

Michael: [*Shouting:*] Give me back my turtle!

Julie: It's *my* turtle! I found it first!

Rosa: Come back here, you two!

[*The children ignore* Rosa *and run out. Rosa picks up the book and puts it back on the dresser, next to a large jewelry box. Then, looking around to be sure no one is watching, she opens the jewelry box and takes out a diamond necklace.*]

Rosa: ¡Qué precioso! [*She holds the necklace against her neck.*] Just like the one in the window of Jewelry World. It must cost a fortune.

[Rosa *hears a noise and quickly puts the necklace back in the box. She picks up the feather duster and starts dusting the book and the dresser as* Mrs. Kelly *enters.*]

Rosa: Oh, hello, Mrs. Kelly. I was just cleaning up.

Mrs. Kelly: I wish you would clean up the kitchen. The breakfast dishes are still in the sink. And I asked you to wax the floor.

Rosa: I'm sorry, Mrs. Kelly. But I was so busy today.

Mrs. Kelly: Well, I suppose you can do it tonight.

Rosa: Oh, please, Mrs. Kelly, not tonight! Tonight is my new ESL class.

Mrs. Kelly: Are you still taking ESL? Your English is good enough.

Rosa: I don't want to be good enough. I want to be perfect!

Mrs. Kelly: I'm sure you do, but I wish you would dust half as well as you speak English! [*She runs her finger along the dresser top, noticing the dust.*] Look, Rosa. This isn't a glamorous job, but we do pay you, and we treat you like one of the family. I know you think you're too good for this job . . .

Rosa: Oh, no, Mrs. Kelly!

Mrs. Kelly: . . . but it *is* a job. And in these times . . .

[Michael *and* Julie *run in again, screaming.*]

Michael: Julie, I'm gonna kill you! You ruined all my baseball cards!

Julie: It's not my fault! It's *your* fault!

Mrs. Kelly: Go to your rooms right now! [Julie *and* Michael *run out. To* Rosa:] Oh, go to your class. But promise me you'll do the kitchen tomorrow.

Rosa: I promise. First thing in the morning! [*The doorbell rings.*] That's Lily. She's going to class with me. [Rosa *takes another look in the mirror, and straightens her skirt.*] Oh, these rags! I wish I had some decent clothes. [*To* Mrs. Kelly:] You're the greatest, Mrs. Kelly! *¡Muchísimas gracias!* Thank you so much!

Mrs. Kelly: *De nada,* I guess. You're welcome. [Rosa *runs off, leaving* Mrs. Kelly *onstage shaking her head.*] Sometimes I wonder why I put up with that girl. [*She goes off.*]

SCENE 2

The ESL classroom. Chairs are set up in a semicircle.

[Lily *and* Rosa *enter and join a group of girls who are standing outside the classroom. There is also a group of boys waiting for class to begin. Each group is watching the other.*]

Roberto: [*To the boys:*] *¡Qué bonita!* Who is that girl? What's her name?

Víctor: Forget it, my friend. Rosa won't even look at you—unless you have just won the lottery.

Roberto: What do you mean?

Víctor: She only cares about *this*. [*He rubs his thumb and first two fingers together—the sign for money.*] Nobody around here is good enough for her. She thinks she's a movie star or something.

Lily: Look, Rosa. Look at that new boy. He can't stop staring at you. Isn't he cute?

Rosa: [*Looking in her compact mirror.*] Yeah, I guess. If you like that type.

Lily: I like that type. Why doesn't he look at *me*? [*She blows a kiss in* Roberto's *direction, then giggles embarrassedly as he turns away. Just then an older man walks by. He tips his hat to the girls as he walks into the classroom.*]

Lily: [*Nudging* Rosa:] You know who that is? [Rosa *shakes her head.*] He owns Jewelry World. My cousin worked for him for six months. He's a slave driver, a real Scrooge McDuck. He makes all the girls live at the factory. They work about 14 hours a day—no breaks, nothing.

Teacher: [*Entering.*] Good evening, everybody. Please come in and sit down. [*Everyone takes a seat.*] Since this is a new semester, I'd like to begin the class with introductions. Please tell us your name and a little about yourself. And I think it would be nice to share a dream you have for the future. Who wants to start?

Lily: [*Raising her hand.*] I will. My name is Lily, and I am from Taiwan. My dream is to learn about computers, so I can work in an office.

Roberto: I am Roberto from Puebla, Mexico. I work at the restaurant across the street. I am a busboy now, but soon I will be a waiter. My dream [*he looks at* Rosa] is to marry a beautiful girl and have many beautiful children.

Mr. Santini: I am from Italia, and I am from the Santini family. We are jewelry makers in the old country, and now I make jewelry here. Jewelry World—that's me. In Italy, I am just a jewelry maker. Here I am the whole *world*! I study English so I can speak to my customers. In business, you have to work hard and not waste time on foolish dreams.

Víctor: Me llamo Víctor. I mean, my name is Víctor. My job is to fix the cars. My hobby is to love the girls. I love them, and they love me. I am *their* dream! [*The girls in the class roll their eyes and groan.*]

Suzi: I am Suzi, from Argentina. I work for a big family and watch their little babies. I miss my family very much. I dream of *them*.

Teacher: Rosa, what about you?

Rosa: Oh, I'm Rosa. I too work for a family. But that's only temporary . . . [*proudly*] because soon I'll have enough money for my school.

Teacher: Oh, Rosa, you're going to the university!

Rosa: University? Oh no! The French Institute of Modeling—that's where I want to go. I want to be a famous model, on the cover of every magazine. That's *my* dream.

Teacher: Thank you, class. That was wonderful! Let's take our break and meet back here in ten minutes.

[Roberto, Víctor, *and* Mr. Santini *surround* Rosa, *who tries to ignore them.*]

Víctor: Hey, Rosa! What kind of pictures are you gonna pose for?

Mr. Santini: Miss Rosa, you are a beautiful girl, like a rose. I give you my card: Joseph Santini, Jewelry World. A pretty girl like you—you could help me in the store. Maybe you could come see me someday. [Rosa *shrugs, takes his card, and all walk offstage.*]

SCENE 3

At the Kellys' house, a few days later.

[Rosa *is reading a fashion magazine.* Michael *and* Julie *are playing catch.* Mrs. Kelly *enters, carrying two heavy shopping bags.*]

Mrs. Kelly: Okay, kids, I told you not to play ball in the house!

Children: Sorry, mom. [*They run out.*]

Mrs. Kelly: Rosa, why weren't you watching them?

Rosa: I *was* watching them, Mrs. Kelly. I just stopped for a minute to check out this article on hairstyles.

Mrs. Kelly: Do you think you could give me a hand with these bags? [*The phone rings.* Mrs. Kelly *puts down the bags and picks up the phone.*] Hello. Yes, just a minute. Rosa, it's for you. It's Roberto again.

Rosa: Not again! [*Into phone.*] Hello. Listen, Roberto. I really don't think you should call me anymore . . . A dinner dance? For a Hollywood movie director? How did *you* get tickets? . . . Your boss? . . . He did? Well, in that case, I would love to be your date! Thank you, Roberto. Goodbye. [*She hangs up, then screams with joy.*] A dinner dance with people from Hollywood! I'm so excited! . . . Oh, no. I can't go! I don't have anything to wear! [*She bursts into tears.*]

Mrs. Kelly: Rosa, please! You're crying all over my dresser! You'll ruin the wood! Look, I'll give you my black cocktail dress. I've only worn it a few times. It'll be perfect for you. [*She takes the dress from the back of a chair and holds it in front of Rosa.*]

Rosa: Oh, Mrs. Kelly, are you sure you want to give me this?

Mrs. Kelly: Only if you stop crying. And I'll tell you what— since this will be a special evening, I'll let you borrow my special necklace. [*She takes the necklace out of the jewelry box and puts it around Rosa's neck.*] There! You look like a princess.

Rosa: I *am* a princess, and you're an angel, Mrs. Kelly. I'll never forget this. Never! [*Rosa runs off, hugging the dress. Mrs. Kelly is left with her shopping bags. She picks them up and exits, shaking her head.*]

SCENE 4

The dinner dance, in the ballroom.

[*Music starts and well-dressed couples begin dancing in. A* Waiter *enters with a tray of champagne.*]

Man #1: Would you like some champagne, darling?

Woman #1: Of course, darling! Nice party, isn't it?

Man # 1: Very nice. [*They drink their champagne in one gulp, hand the* Waiter *their empty glasses, and continue dancing.* Roberto *and* Rosa *cross the stage in front of the dance scene.* Rosa *is wearing an old coat over her borrowed dress and necklace.*]

Rosa: Listen to that music, Roberto! I can't wait to start dancing! Ooo, just a minute! I can't wear this coat inside. It's too ugly. Will you hold it for me?

Roberto: Sure, *princesa.*

Rosa: I'm so nervous. How do I look?

Roberto: Like a star. A real star, from heaven. [*They enter the scene,* Rosa *looking and feeling like a star.*]

Man #2: Mmm. Very pretty. [*Watching* Rosa, *he accidentally pours his champagne on* Woman #2.]

Woman #2: Richard! Look what you're doing!

Man #2: Oh! Sorry, dear!

Woman #3: Who is that girl?

Man #3: I don't know, but I intend to find out. [*He approaches* Rosa.] Excuse me. May I have this dance?

Rosa: Certainly.

[*They begin dancing. After a few seconds,* Man #2 *cuts in.*]

Man # 2:   Hello, gorgeous.

Rosa: Do you know the fox-trot?

Man #2:   Are you kidding? Ask my grandfather—or *his* grandfather. They used to dance stuff like that. This is the 90s, baby! [*He twirls her around.* Man #1 *cuts in. As the men take turns dancing with* Rosa, Roberto *watches. He is beginning to get angry.*]

Roberto: Rosa, when is *my* turn to dance with you?

Rosa: Please, Roberto. Can't you see I'm having fun?

Roberto: But I'm the one who brought you here. You're supposed to dance with me!

Rosa: Stop acting like a child. You can dance with me later.

[Man#1 *takes* Rosa*'s hand and she dances off with him.*]

Roberto: Víctor was right. I should forget you. You may be pretty, but you have a refrigerator for a heart. Goodbye, Rosa.

Rosa: Roberto, wait! [*He goes off.*]

Man #1:   Let him go, honey. He's not your type. A girl like you deserves the best. Listen, if you're ever in Los Angeles, look me up. I'll take you to lunch.

Waiter: Ladies and gentlemen, dinner is served on the terrace.

Man #1:   I'll take you to dinner right now. [*He offers* Rosa *his arm. Everyone exits, laughing and talking.*]

SCENE 5

The dinner dance, in the lobby.

[*After a moment,* Rosa *reenters. She looks very happy.*]

Rosa: This is the best night of my life! What beautiful food! What beautiful people! And I'm one of them! [*Admiring herself in an imaginary full-length mirror, she puts on fresh lipstick. Suddenly she touches her neck, discovering with horror that her necklace is gone.*] Oh, no! My necklace! It's gone! I must find it!

[*She runs frantically around the stage, desperately trying to find her necklace. Then she goes into the audience, asking members of the audience: "Have you seen it? Have you seen my necklace?" Offstage, there is a burst of laughter and the sound of cheerful conversation as* Rosa *gradually realizes the necklace is gone for good. She is heartbroken.*]

Rosa: I can't find it anywhere. What am I going to do? I can't go home without it . . . Mr. Santini. I must have his card in my purse.

[*She walks slowly over to a telephone and dials. Across the stage, another phone rings.* Mr. Santini *enters in his bathrobe and answers it.*]

Mr. Santini: Hello. Who is this?

Rosa: Mr. Santini, it's Rosa. I'm sorry to call you so late, but this is an emergency. I'm in trouble, and you're the only one who can help.

Mr. Santini: Rosa?

Rosa: Rosa, from the English class. Mr. Santini, I've got to buy the diamond necklace in your store window. Right now.

Mr. Santini: [*Laughs.*] That necklace costs more than $5,000. You have that much money?

Rosa: No, but I'll work for it, I promise. I'll come and work for you until I pay it off.

Mr. Santini: You'll have to work hard to pay all that money back. I only pay minimum wage.

Rosa: I know.

Mr. Santini: And no days off.

Rosa: I know.

Mr. Santini: And room and board—I deduct for that.

Rosa: I know, I know. I'll live in the factory. I'll do anything.

Mr. Santini: I'll meet you at the shop in a half-hour. You sign a paper for me, and I'll give you the necklace. Okay?

Rosa: Okay. [*She hangs up the phone.*] My life is over. [*She exits, slowly and sadly.*]

SCENE 6

The Kelly house, late that night.

[Rosa *tiptoes in. She is wearing the necklace again, but she still looks very unhappy.*]

Mrs. Kelly: [*From offstage.*] Rosa? Is that you? [*She enters, wearing a long robe and slippers.*]

Rosa: Mrs. Kelly, I didn't mean to wake you.

Mrs. Kelly: Well, did you have a good time?

Rosa: It was better than good. It was wonderful. But now I have to say goodbye.

Mrs. Kelly: Goodbye? I don't understand.

Rosa: The director offered me a part in his new movie. He wants me to come to Hollywood tomorrow. I'm sorry, but I have to leave in the morning.

Mrs. Kelly: You don't look very happy. Are you sure you're all right?

Rosa: [*Trying to smile.*] I'm fine. I've never been happier. Thank you for the necklace, Mrs. Kelly. It changed my life.

Mrs. Kelly: Good luck, Rosa.

Rosa: Goodbye, Mrs. Kelly. [*She exits.*]

Mrs. Kelly: [*Sighing.*] I guess it's no use asking her to do the dishes before she leaves. And I just had my nails done, too! [*She exits.*]

SCENE 7

Santini's Jewelry World.

[*We hear "September Song," "As Time Goes By," "Those Were the Days, My Friend," or some other song about time passing as* Mr. Santini *enters, tearing months off a calendar. He looks at his watch.*]

Mr. Santini: 7:15 and I'm the only one at work. Where is that girl? [*Calling offstage:*] Rosa! Rosa! Where are you?

Rosa: [*From offstage:*] Coming! Coming, Mr. Santini!

[Rosa *enters, looking tired and much less glamorous than before. She is wearing glasses and a shapeless work-shirt and holding a heavy bracelet. She yawns and stretches.*]

Mr. Santini: What's the matter with you, you lazy girl? Don't I pay you to be on the job at 7 A.M.?

Rosa: [*Tiredly.*] I'm sorry, Mr. Santini. I was working on Mrs. Schneider's bracelet till 3 in the morning. You said she needed it right away.

Mr. Santini: Let me see what you did. [*As Rosa hands him the bracelet, he looks at her critically.*] Look at you! If you don't start taking care of yourself, I'll have to put you in the back of the shop where the customers can't see you! [*He examines the bracelet.*] Well, at least your work is getting better. Here, fix this necklace. [*He tosses a necklace on the table.*]

Rosa: Yes, Mr. Santini.

Mr. Santini: And watch what you're doing. Mrs. Burton is very particular.

Rosa: [*She sighs.*] Of course, Mr. Santini. [*Mr. Santini goes off, and* Rosa *begins working on the necklace. It is difficult work and demands all her concentration. She squints as she handles the small jeweler's tools and doesn't notice when* Roberto *enters, dressed in a suit and tie.*]

Roberto: Excuse me, miss. I'd like to have my watch repaired.

Rosa: [*Looking up from her work and recognizing him.*] Roberto!

Roberto: You know me?

Rosa: It's me, Rosa. Rosa López.

Roberto: [*Shocked.*] Rosa? I didn't recognize you. You look so different!

Rosa: [*Smiling sadly.*] Yes, I guess I do.

Roberto: I thought you went to that school for models. When you didn't come back to English class, we all expected to see you on TV or something. What happened?

Rosa: I had a little change of plans. After that dinner dance you took me to. Remember?

Roberto: That was almost two years ago.

Rosa: Only two years? It seems like twenty.

Roberto: Have you been here the whole time?

Rosa: Right here in Jewelry World. Just me and Mr. Santini.

Roberto: How come?

Rosa: It's a long story. But it's almost over. I've almost paid it off.

Roberto: Paid *what* off?

Rosa: I'll tell you all about it some day. But what about you? How are you, Roberto?

Roberto: I'm still at the restaurant. But I'm not a busboy any-more. I'm the manager.

Rosa: Oh, Roberto, I'm so happy for you.

Roberto: Look, Rosa, I hate to rush you, but I really need that watch. Can you fix it for me?

Rosa: Oh, sure. [*She fixes it while he watches.*] Here it is. As good as new.

Roberto: Great. How much do I owe you?

Rosa: Nothing. It's on the house.

Roberto: You don't have to do that.

Rosa: Please. I want to.

Roberto: Well, thanks a lot. [*Looking at his watch.*] I've got to go. Maybe we can have dinner together sometime.

Rosa: I'd like that.

Roberto: I'll call you. Thanks again for the watch.

[*As he leaves,* Mr. Santini *enters, shouting.*]

Mr. Santini: What did you do, you foolish girl? You fixed that watch for nothing! This is a business, not a charity!

Rosa: I'm sorry, Mr. Santini. He was an old friend. You can take it out of my salary.

Mr. Santini: You bet I will! Foolish girl! You'll never get any-where in life! In business, we have no time for friends! . . . Now fix that necklace! [*He goes off, muttering to himself. Rosa begins to work on the necklace again. After a moment,* Mrs. Kelly *enters.*]

Mrs. Kelly: [*Softly.*] Rosa? Is that you, Rosa?

Rosa: [*Looking up.*] Mrs. Kelly? This is really a day for reunions! Roberto was just here this morning.

Mrs. Kelly: I know. I ran into him down the street. My poor Rosa! How you've changed!

Rosa: Yes, I've had a hard time since I saw you last. And all because of you.

Mrs. Kelly: Because of me? What do you mean?

Rosa: Do you remember that diamond necklace you once lent me?

Mrs. Kelly: Of course. What about it?

Rosa: Well, I lost it.

Mrs. Kelly: You lost it? But you gave it back to me.

Rosa: I bought you another one just like it. From this store. I've been paying it off for almost two years now. Maybe $5,000 doesn't seem like a lot to you, but I had to earn every penny of it.

Mrs. Kelly: You mean you bought a diamond necklace to replace mine?

Rosa: Yes. You never noticed? [*She smiles proudly.*] I thought they looked the same.

Mrs. Kelly: Oh, my poor Rosa! That necklace of mine wasn't real. Those were fake diamonds—just pieces of glass. The whole thing wasn't worth $50!

Rosa: [*Shocked.*] $50!

Mrs. Kelly: If only you had told me before!

Rosa: [*Again, as if she can't understand what she has just heard.*] $50! [*Suddenly, she begins to laugh.*] It's funny, isn't it? I worked for two years to pay for a $50 necklace! I guess the joke is on me.

Mrs. Kelly: I'll sell the necklace. You can have the money. You can go to your modeling school.

Rosa: Now? I don't think so. But I could use the money for school. I'm used to hard work now. I think I'd like to go to college.

Mrs. Kelly: Rosa, come home with me. You can have your old room back. You'll have plenty of time to study.

Rosa: And dust! Wait till you see how well I can dust now, Mrs. Kelly. I've had lots of practice. [*They begin to walk off together as* Mr. Santini *enters.*]

Mr. Santini: [*Shouting.*] Rosa! Rosa! Come back here! You didn't finish with the necklace!

Rosa: [*Calling back over her shoulder.*] Oh, yes I did, Mr. Santini. I'm finished with it for good! [*She exits with* Mrs. Kelly.]

Mr. Santini: [*Angrily.*] That's what I get for being too nice to her! [*He pounds his fist on the table.*] Now I've got to finish the work myself. Just as well. She never could have done it well enough, that lazy girl! In business, you want a job done right, you've got to do it yourself. [*He sits down and begins working on the necklace, muttering to himself, as . . . the play ends.*]

REVIEWS

THE WAY IT WAS

The cartoons show all the events in *The Necklace,* but not in the order they took place. Number the events in the correct order. The first one is done for you.

__1__   Instead of working, Rosa practices her English and admires the necklace in Mrs. Kelly's bedroom.

_____   The students discuss their dreams for the future.

_____ At the dance, all the men admire Rosa.

_____ Rosa learns the truth about the necklace and leaves her job at Jewelry World to begin a new life.

_____ Roberto leaves the dance, angry that Rosa is ignoring him.

_____ Rosa works long hours for Mr. Santini to pay for the necklace.

_____ Mrs. Kelly lets Rosa go to her English class with her work unfinished.

_____ Mrs. Kelly lends Rosa a dress and necklace for the dance.

_____ After a wonderful evening, Rosa loses the necklace and calls Mr. Santini to arrange to buy a replacement.

_____ Roberto calls Rosa and invites her to a dinner dance.

PREPOSITIONS: LITTLE WORDS THAT MEAN A LOT

Prepositions are some of the hardest words to get right. But you can do it! In each of the sentences below, circle the correct preposition. The first one is done for you.

at	in front of	off
along	in	out of
around	on	over
behind		

1. Rosa admires herself (in, on) the mirror.

2. Rosa balances a book (in, on) her head. The children knock it (off, over).

3. Mrs. Kelly runs her finger (along, around) the dresser to check for dust.

4. Mrs. Kelly takes the necklace (out of, off) her jewelry box and puts it (along, around) Rosa's neck.

5. She holds the dress (along, in front of) Rosa.

6. Rosa wears an old coat (on, over) her borrowed dress.

7. Mr. Santini expects Rosa to be (in, at) work by 7:15.

8. Roberto is surprised to see Rosa (behind, around) the counter (at, on) the jewelry store.

CONTRACTIONS: THEY'RE EASY!

In spoken English, we rarely say *cannot* when we can say *can't* or *do not* when we can say *don't*. Contractions make speech sound more natural—and shorter! Below are the long forms of some dialogue found in *The Necklace*. See if you can shorten each sentence with the correct contraction. The first one is done for you.

1. What is that?

   What's that?

2. I had better look it up.

3. She is wearing the latest fashion from Paris.

4. It is my turtle.

5. You are welcome.

6. Is he not cute?

7. Why does he not look at me?

8. I would like to begin the class with introductions.

_____

9. Let us take our break.

_____

10. Why were you not watching them?

_____

11. I cannot go.

_____

12. I do not have anything to wear.

_____

13. I am sorry.

_____

14. I did not mean to wake you.

_____

15. It is funny, is it not?

_____

WHO SAID IT?

Match each character with his or her line from *The Necklace.*

Rosa

Mrs. Kelly

Man at the dance

Roberto

(*continued on the next page*)

Mr. Santini

_____ **1.** "I know you think you're too good for this job."

_____ **2.** "In business you have to work hard and not waste time on foolish dreams."

_____ **3.** "You may be pretty, but you have a refrigerator for a heart."

_____ **4.** "What beautiful people! And I'm one of them!"

_____ **5.** "A girl like you deserves the best."

RHYME TIME

Words that rhyme are words that sound alike, such as *that* and *hat*, *stop* and *top*, *around* and *found*. In each of the columns below, all words rhyme except one. Circle the word that does not rhyme with the others. The first one is done for you.

thick	seen	wear	know	brought
quick	in	her	go	bought
pick	clean	hair	now	thought
(speak)	mean	there	show	toward

bump	laugh	run	new	store
some	rough	ran	do	for
come	half	fun	too	star
dumb	calf	won	so	door

Now choose a partner and practice saying the words aloud to each other. Can you hear the rhymes? Can you hear the not-rhymes?

LET'S DANCE!

Rosa is invited to an elegant dinner dance and has the time of her life. When was the last time you went out dancing? What kind of place was it? With whom did you go? Did you enjoy it?

Do you like to dance, or do you just like to watch other people dance? What kind of dancing do you like best? Are dancing parties common in your native country?

ROLE PLAY

Using your memories and your imagination, choose a partner and act out a scene between two people at a dance. In preparing your scene, be sure to answer the following questions:

Who **are you?**   Are you acquaintances, a married couple, friends meeting by chance, strangers meeting for the first time? How old are you? What kind of people are you? How are you dressed?

Where **are you?**   Are you at a nightclub, a private party, a church social, a folk dance festival, a country/western bar? Is there a live band or recorded music? What kind of music is playing? What town or country are you in?

What **do you think of each other?**   Do you like or not like each other? Are you in love, angry, or bored with each other?

Why are you here?   Were you invited, or did you come to meet someone? Do you especially like the place or the people?

When did you come?   Have you been here for hours, or did you just get here? What time of day—or night—is it?

How do you like the dance?   Are you having fun? Do you dance well together, or are you awkward and uncomfortable? Is the music too loud, too soft, or just the way you like it?

It may not be necessary to say all these things in words. You can show a lot about your character with gestures and facial expressions. In acting, as in real life, "actions speak louder than words," so don't be afraid to dance if you feel like it!

BACKSTORY

Good actors know their characters inside and out. They know exactly what happened to make them the way they are. In the mind of the playwright, every character has a *backstory*—a life before the play begins.

Choose one of the characters in *The Necklace* and develop a backstory for him or her by answering the following questions *in the character's own voice.*

Where were you born and raised?

What was your childhood like?

What do you like to do in your spare time?

Who are the members of your family, and what do they do?

What kind of house do you live in?

Who is your best friend?

Of course, you can choose one of the major characters, like Mrs. Kelly or Rosa. But don't forget the minor characters—they can be fun to work with too. Be as creative as you like—but be sure that your answers really fit the character you have chosen.

INTERVIEW

When you have answered the six Backstory questions, pick a partner. Ask your partner the same questions, and let him or her answer *in character*. Use the space below to make notes—even the best interviewers can't remember everything! Can you guess which character your partner has chosen?

Now let your partner ask you the questions. Can your partner guess which character you are?

Write a short biography of *your partner's character,* based on what you learned in the interview.

KEY WORDS AND EXPRESSIONS: REVIEW

Below you will find a short summary of *The Necklace.* Fill in the blanks with the words and expressions you have already learned.

deserves	heartbroken	lazy
fake	How come?	look him up
give her a hand	is not her type	put up with
glamorous	(It) costs a fortune	recognize

In *The Necklace,* Rosa is an attractive but rather

_____ young woman who works as a house-

keeper but dreams of a _____ career as a

model. Whenever her boss, Mrs. Kelly, asks Rosa to _____

_____ , Rosa is busy doing something else. Why does Mrs.

Kelly _____ Rosa's behavior? It's hard to tell.

But when Rosa is invited to an elegant dinner dance by Roberto,

Mrs. Kelly lends her a beautiful necklace that Rosa is sure

_____ .

At the dance, everyone admires Rosa. One man asks her to

_____ in Los Angeles and assures her that

poor Roberto _____ ; she _____

the best. After a wonderful evening, Rosa is _____

when she discovers she has lost the borrowed necklace.

In order to buy a replacement, she arranges to go to work for Mr.

Santini, a jeweler. Hard work changes her, and when Roberto

comes into the jewelry store, he doesn't even _____

her. That same day, Mrs. Kelly drops by, and Rosa discovers that

the original necklace was only a _____ . At the

end, she leaves the store with Mrs. Kelly to begin a new life.

JUST FOR FUN

All the words below are from *The Necklace*, and all of them begin with "B." Fill in the blanks to complete each word. Then use the numbered letters to form the final answer.

Small child; sweetheart	B __ B __	
	1	
Something lent	B __ __ __ __ __ __ __	
Paper sack for groceries	B __ __	
Someone who cleans tables	B __ __ B __ __	
Lovely	B __ __ __ __ __ __ __ __	
		2
Employer	B __ __ __	
Hit into accidentally	B __ __ __ into	
Return	give B __ __ __	
		3
Occupied (with work)	B __ __ __	
First meal of the day	B __ __ __ __ __ __ __ __	
	4	

Answer:

(What the necklace was:)   __ __ __ __
　　　　　　　　　　　　　　 2　1　3　4

WRITE IT, DON'T FIGHT IT!

The Necklace is divided into the seven scenes listed below. Next to each scene, write a brief description of what happens. The first one is done for you.

Scene 1: A room in the Kelly house.

Instead of doing the housework, Rosa practices her English and admires Mrs. Kelly's necklace. Mrs. Kelly returns and is upset that Rosa has neglected her work, but lets her go to her ESL class anyway.

Scene 2: The ESL classroom.

Scene 3: At the Kelly's house, a few days later.

Scene 4: The dinner dance, in the ballroom.

Scene 5: The dinner dance, in the lobby.

Scene 6: The Kelly house, late that night.

Scene 7: Santini's Jewelry World.

YOU BE THE PLAYWRIGHT!

At the end of *The Necklace,* Rosa goes home with Mrs. Kelly. What do you think happens next? Does she go to college—and graduate? What kind of career does she choose? How long does she stay with Mrs. Kelly? Does she go out with Roberto again? Does she ever get married? Can you imagine Rosa at age 40, perhaps with children of her own?

Choose one of these possibilities or any other that comes to your mind and write a short sequel to *The Necklace.*

SOMETHING TO THINK ABOUT

1. Rosa has a job, but she thinks being a model would be much more glamorous. Are some jobs really glamorous? What's your idea of a glamorous job, and why?

2. Why doesn't Rosa tell Mrs. Kelly that she lost the necklace? What might have happened if she had told her immediately?

3. Do you like Rosa better at the beginning or at the end of the play? Why?

4. Mr. Santini might be called the "villain" of the play. Do you agree? What are some of his good points?

5. If you were in Rosa's English class, how would you introduce yourself? What dream for the future would you share?

GLOSSARY

(It) costs a fortune. It is very expensive.

deserve earn or have the right to something

de nada (Sp.) It's nothing. (You're welcome.)

fake not real

give someone a hand help someone

glamorous fascinating and beautiful

heartbroken very unhappy

How come? Why?

lazy dislike work

Look me up. Come visit me.

Me llamo . . . (Sp.) My name is . . .

¡Muchísimas gracias! (Sp.) Thank you so much!

(He's/she's) not your type. He/she is not your kind of person.

princesa (Sp.) princess

put up with (someone or something) don't let a person or situation bother you

¡Qué bonita eres! (Sp.) How pretty you are!

¡Qué precioso! (Sp.) How beautiful!

recognize remember knowing someone or something from before